Articles for Personal Growth and Development Volume I
By
Brenda Diann Johnson

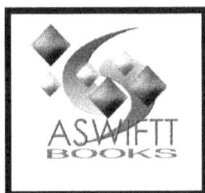

ASWIFTT ENTERPRISES, LLC
Duncanville, Texas 75138

Brenda Diann Johnson
brendadiannjohnson@yahoo.com

Published by
ASWIFTT ENTERPRISES, LLC
Imprint: ASWIFTT BOOKS
P.O. Box 380669
Duncanville, Texas 75138

ISBN: 978-0-9847015-2-0

Library of Congress Control Number: 2012902776

Printed in the United States of America.

All scripture quotations are from the King James Version of the Bible unless otherwise noted. All definitions are from The Random House College Dictionary, Revised Edition unless otherwise noted.

Cover Design and Editing by Brenda Diann Johnson

Dedications

I dedicate this book to my two beautiful girls, Diamond and Kamille. It is my prayer you will continue to seek knowledge, obtain wisdom and pursue the purpose God has ordained for you.

Table of Contents

Introduction

Personal Growth and Development means to grow into a more mature and advanced state. (Random House College Dictionary) All human beings were born into this world as infants. The process of physical growth and development took place over many years until we developed into adults. The same growth and development takes place when it comes to mental maturity. We started learning things formally and informally as children and it continued to adulthood. Education from elementary, middle school, high school and then college prepared us for the challenges of today. When we continue to educate ourselves formally or informally it helps us with our personal growth and development.

"Articles for Personal Growth and Development: Volume I" is a collection of articles that were written and published by Brenda Diann Johnson. These articles are literary pieces that are dear to the author's heart. These articles include lessons learned by the author and information the author feels is worthy to share.

"Articles for Personal Growth and Development: Volume I" includes topics about Time Management, Selfishness, Dreams, Goals and more. These articles will encourage you in areas of strengths and will motivate you to improve in areas of weakness. Continue to look for more upcoming articles by Brenda Diann Johnson.

It's Up To You To Get Your Dreams and Goals Moving!

Article I:
It's Up To You To Get Your Dreams and Goals Moving!

"What are you waiting on?" Again, I say "What are you waiting on?" The earth realm is waiting for you to release the talents and abilities God gave you. At the moment of your conception, God gave you talents and abilities to one day share with the human race.

Faith without works is dead according to the Bible in James chapter 2 verse 20. In James chapter 2 verse 17 it states, Even so faith, if it has not works, is dead, being alone. In these examples, it is clear your faith and works are necessary to make things happen.

In Hebrews chapter 11 verse 1, the Bible defines faith as the substance of things hoped for, the evidence of things not seen. In the Random House College Dictionary, faith is the confidence or trust in a person or thing or the occurrence of a future event. Your motivation to get moving is your faith or belief that your dreams and goals can and will happen.

According to Dictionary.com, works are defined as exertion or effort directed to produce or accomplish something. Works are your labor or toil. Your works are what you do or what actions you take to get things done.

Many people wonder why they never accomplish their dreams or goals. Some continue to use the old popular saying "I am waiting for my ship to come in." What ship are you talking about? Your goals and dreams will never happen if you don't **sow labor into time.** This is the same concept when you sow or plant seeds into the ground. You won't receive a harvest of fruits and vegetables if you don't sow seeds into the ground. The same principle applies if you don't sow labor or effort into time. You won't see the accomplishments or results of your dreams and goals.

Your accomplishments or results of your dreams and goals start with a PLAN. The Random House College Dictionary states a plan is a method of action or procedure. In a plan you write down what you will do to make your dreams and goals a reality. Your plan is your road map to get to your desired destination.

Sit down and thoroughly think about what accomplishments and results you want from your dreams and goals. You will have a visual guide when you write out your plan. Your visual guide will lead you in the direction you want to go. Your visual guide will also keep you from losing your way or straying off your path.

Make the decision to get your dreams and goals moving. Today's decision will yield results sooner than later. When you procrastinate it delays your dreams and goals. If you are struggling with procrastination, Steve Pavlina list the root causes of procrastination and he also gives practical tools to overcome procrastination on stevepavlina.com.

Don't deny the Earth realm or the human race any longer of your talents and abilities. Begin to sow labor into time each day towards your dreams and goals. You will reap the fruits of your labor when you continue to **Sow Labor Into Time**.

Time Management Is Always a Hot Topic Up For Discussion

Article II:
Time Management
Is Always a Hot Topic
Up For Discussion

Learning how to manage time on a daily basis is a challenge for many and seems to be easy for some. Time Management is when you get to choose how to spend your time. You plan every hour, minute and second of how, when and where you will divide 24 hours. You can also prioritize your time to make sure you accomplish your tasks. The things that are most important to you should have the highest ranking on your schedule.

According to Wikipedia.com, time management is the act or process of exercising conscious control over the amount of time spent on specific activities, especially to increase efficiency or productivity.

The key to efficiency and productivity is making sure you use your time wisely. Making sure time does not slip away without a stamp of productivity and accomplishment. There are many ways to manage time and the key is to find what works best for you.

Some people manage their time by writing down "to do lists" and some write things down on daily, weekly and monthly calendars called planners.

There are other creative ways like putting things on sticky notes, keeping journals, pop up reminders on computer calendars, etc. Whatever method you choose, make sure it is effective and productive for you.

The most effective and productive system that has worked for me over the years is a combination of writing "to do lists" and planners. I write everything down. I do this habitually, so I won't forget anything. When you are busy and have a lot of tasks, it is easy to forget something. It is always best to write things down. I also use daily and monthly planners. I started using the Franklin Covey Planner system when I took the class "What Matters Most" in 2001.

I always have a feeling of accomplishment and satisfaction when I get things done. When I plan out my time daily and monthly it helps me stay on track with my goals. My focus is then on purpose. Each day I only focus on what is planned on my daily schedule while leaving room for those things I don't have control over. This is important because sometimes unfortunate things happen even when things are well planned out.

Sometimes unfortunate things can cause some goals to go uncompleted for a period of time. In these instances, don't blame yourself, stay on track and pray for wisdom on how you should proceed.

In the month of November, I start planning my monthly calendars for the next year. I include new goals and old goals in my planning. I also celebrate the goals and tasks I completed in the previous year. This shows how much I accomplished.

The old adage "Time Waits for No Man" is true and should be taken seriously. Time goes on no matter what. You cannot roll back time. Once time has moved on, it has moved on. This may sound depressing for some but there is hope on redeeming time. According to Ephesians 5: 15, 16 we are to be careful how we walk, not as unwise but as wise, making the most of our time because the days are evil. (ASV)

In the Random House College Dictionary, redeem means to buy back, recover or to make up for. When you have lost time on a task, you must find a way to redeem the time to complete the task.

Some people recover time by doubling up on tasks, delegating tasks and using technology. Other people resort to methods used by college students by pulling all nighters without any sleep. In Garfield Gates article "Effective Study Habits for College Students" in Hub Pages, he gives 7 tips on how college students can study effectively and plan ahead. He also covers some time management tips for students.

In Randy Morrison's CD series "Time: The Currency of a Prosperous Life," he says that God created us to have dreams and goals and it will take time to make them become a reality. He also says that the major difference between the prosperous and the poor is their value of time.

Managing your time will always be important. Time management is the key to getting things done. The way you manage time will determine how much you achieve in a given day, week, month or year. Finding the best time management system that works for you is essential in moving forward with your goals and dreams.

Your Purpose Should Dictate How You Spend Your Time

Article III:
Your Purpose Should Dictate How You Spend Your Time

You don't have time to waste or squander. Your time is valuable, precious and limited. Make the best choices concerning your time each day. Choose what yields the greatest results when it comes to your time.

Start by writing a mission statement for your life. A mission statement highlights your intended purpose on Planet Earth. Your mission statement should include your talents, abilities and skills you want to contribute to the world. A mission statement will keep you focused. It will also help you be decisive about how you spend your time.

Your mission statement should be used to create the tasks to accomplish your goals. It takes time and energy to see the results of your goals. Time spent on endeavors that are not related to your purpose is time lost or wasted.

According to Habakkuh 2:2, a vision should be written and made plain upon tables, that he may run that readest it. Your mission statement is the written purpose or vision for your life.

Developing a mission statement for your life helps you feel empowered. It helps you strategically move forward in accomplishing your goals. Your written purpose, however, does not keep you from encountering people who compete for your time and energy. Your time and energy should be spent to fulfill your purpose. Extra time should be used to volunteer to others. It's nothing wrong with helping others. Always remember that charity starts at home.

In the article, "Success Formula! Avoid 10 Most Important Time Stealers" on Bukisa.com, Kamla Joshi lists the inability to say "No!" The struggle to say "No" is when you try to please people. You put what's important to you aside to please someone else. Kamla Joshi says the five deadliest words that rob you of your time are from drop in visitors who say "Have you got a minute?" Kamla Joshi further states that knowing how to deal with interruptions is one of the best skills you can learn.

Eric Garner also talks about managing interruptions in his article "Say No To Time Stealers" on Articlesbase.com. He says learn to be brief because in business your time is your money. He further states that wasting time with unnecessary long meetings with others is a way to let money trickle down the drain.

Using a planner is one way you can account for your time. It also helps when your schedule is in sync with your purpose. A planner helps you account for every second, minute and hour of your day. You can use daily, weekly and monthly planners. A planner can also serve as a record keeper to show how you spent your time for the year.

Before you waste another second, minute or hour, draft your life's mission statement. Think about your talents, abilities and skills. What purpose do you feel you serve on Planet Earth? When you know your purpose, you have clear direction. A mission statement helps you maximize on how you spend your time.

A Truthful Evaluation of Yourself Gives Feedback for Growth and Success

Article IV:
A Truthful Evaluation of Yourself Gives Feedback for Growth and Success

Did you know you were fearfully and wonderfully made by God? (Psalm 139:14) You were created in His image. (Genesis 1:26) You are more than a conqueror. (Romans 8:37) You can do all things through Christ who strengthens you. (Philippians 4:13) Knowing these truths gives you an absolute standard for your life. They are encouragement to your soul.

When you know the truth about God and your existence, confusion is not an option. Be firm, truthful and sure about who you are and what you stand for. Don't let the opinions and prejudices of others tell your story. You are unique, valuable and have a lot to offer. When you know the truth about yourself no one can easily offend or discourage you.

A truthful evaluation of yourself is when you can admit your strengths and weaknesses. No one has to tell you where you are lacking. You know where you need to improve and where you excel. When you continue to truthfully evaluate yourself you continue to grow and mature. When you mature in your weak areas you begin to succeed where you previously failed.

A truthful evaluation also helps you have a balanced view about yourself. You remain level-headed and humble. You are confident in what you can do and ask for help in your areas of weakness. In Chuck Gallozzi's article "Personal Strengths and Weaknesses" posted on Personal-Development.com, he says "It is only when we give equal weight to our strong points and faults that we can realize our potential."

When you know the difference in your strengths and weaknesses you feel good about yourself. You can honestly agree or disagree with someone's report about you without malice. You are not vulnerable to negative criticism. "No one can make you feel inferior without your consent." (Eleanor Roosevelt)

In the article "Personal Strengths and Weaknesses" Chuck Gallozzi also advises to choose friends carefully. He says each relationship nurtures our strengths and weaknesses. He further states that we will either get better or worse depending on the people we choose to spend time with.

Surround yourself with people who have your best interest at heart. They tell you the truth and give balanced advice. Constructive criticism is only good when the underlying motive seeks to help and not destroy. When someone gives you constructive criticism always take what you can use to better yourself and throw away what does not help or pertain to you.

Knowing the truth about yourself also gives you a fair view of others. You can be patient with others because everyone has strengths and weaknesses. No one is perfect and everyone needs improvement in areas of weakness.

It is empowering when you are confident in who you are and what you stand for. No one's comments can make you dislike yourself. You are your greatest ally. Your own support is imperative to your success. You have to believe in yourself even when others do not. Continue to pursue those things that make you a better person. "You are the most influential person you will talk to all day." (Zig Ziglar of Ziglar, Inc.)

Selfishness Stops the Flow of Blessings to You and Others

Article V:
Selfishness Stops the Flow of Blessings to You and Others

Are you making a difference by helping others? Do you feel good when someone's need is met because of you? Helping others when they have a problem or need is a form of charity. Showing grace and mercy to someone in need are acts of unselfish behavior.

Selfishness according to The Random House College Dictionary means devoted to or caring only for oneself; concerned only with one's own interests. Imagine if we lived in a world where everyone practiced selfishness. Imagine if no one cared for another human being and people only looked out for themselves. The Planet Earth would truly be a cold place to live.

In William H. Cole's article "Is Selfishness Healthy?" on Articlesbase.com, he says "Selfish people are like children in that they have not yet learned to balance giving with taking." He further states selfish people feel deprived of something. This deprivation may exist in either their consciousness or in their subconscious mind. They believe that they got "the wrong end of the stick" and now someone or everyone owes them payback.

Even though there are some who practice selfishness daily, for the most part people show acts of grace and mercy. Grace and mercy are shown by people during hurricanes, tornados and earthquake disasters. People also show acts of grace and mercy during economic depressions and wars. Organizations like the American Red Cross, Salvation Army, Samaritan's Purse and Operation Blessing were formed for this very purpose.

When people are unselfish the flow of blessings are continuous. There are continuous transactions of giving and receiving. You see people helping people. Helping others gives you a feeling of making a difference. Your conscience is clear and free from guilt. You recognize it is only by the grace of God you are spared from certain hardships.

Unselfishness allows God to work through people. God is able to answer someone's prayer because of the obedience of another. When you are selfish it stops the flow of blessings to you and others. It stops the blessing to others because God is unable to meet someone's need through you. Your selfishness also keeps you from sowing a seed into someone's life which prevents you from a blessing.

Sowing and reaping is a natural and spiritual law. Farmers use the sowing and reaping principle when they sow seed into the ground and reap a harvest. If the farmer does not plant seed, he cannot expect to get a harvest. It is just that simple. The sowing and reaping principle works the same way in the spiritual.

According to the Bible in Galatians 6:7, it says "Be not deceived; God is not mocked: for whatsoever a man soweth, that shall he also reap." Natural and spiritual laws automatically come to pass whether we want them to or not. When sowing either in the natural or spiritual, make sure what you sow will produce a harvest you want to reap.

Learning to be unselfish is one of the greatest lessons you can learn in life. It helps you have compassion for others. We are responsible for making a difference in our communities and for leaving a legacy. We need to be a solution to someone's problem and a blessing to someone in need. Your unselfish acts of kindness are seeds sown to produce a harvest in your own time of need.

Investigate Before Giving Parental or Adult Consent!

Article VI:
Investigate Before Giving Parental or Adult Consent!

Parental or adult consent is the green-light, the approval signature and the "OK" sign given to minors when they request to do something. Parents and Adults are responsible for ensuring the safety of kids. Minors rely on parents and adults to make the right decisions for them. Parental or adult consent should be valued and never given to minors before investigation.

Parents and adults are responsible by law to protect minors in their possession. There are many dangers and vices that exist in our society today. Some of the dangers and vices did not exist years ago. Teenagers struggle with peer pressure to partake in drugs, alcohol, sex, violence, gangs, etc. Parents and adults should be cautious before giving minors their consent to participate in any event or activity.

Parents and Adults serve as role models and road maps to kids. Minors are unaware of the tricks and schemes that predators use to entice and trap their victims. Sometimes predators use other minors to set a trap for an unsuspecting soul.

Some kids want permission to follow the latest trends to get approval from their peers. Others rebel against the rules and regulations of their parents because their peers don't have the same restrictions.

They feel the grass is greener at their friend's house. Some parents feel pressured to give their kids consent to participate in unapproved activities.

Rearing children in today's society is very complex. Parents must stay in the "Know" of unsafe teenage behavior and trends. Teenagers are in between childhood and adulthood. They are not mature enough to participate in some activities and are responsible enough to do others. It is a parent's responsibility to monitor their child's maturity level.

In Jeanie Davis article, "10 Parenting Tips for Raising Teenagers" posted on WebMD.com, she says parents should give their teenagers a game plan when they are faced with an unsafe situation. She also says parents should help teens figure out solutions to potential problems that may arise when out with friends. Empower your teenager with solid alternatives to follow when approached by the wrong crowd.

Davis further states in her article that parents should talk to their teens about risks that could happen. Discussing the worst-case scenarios with teens helps them make better choices. There will also be times when teenagers rebel and make bad choices. Davis says that parents should let their kids feel guilty. She says that people should feel bad if they have hurt someone or done something wrong. She also says kids need to feel bad sometimes and guilt is a healthy emotion.

As parents and adults, it is our job to make sure kids grow up to be all God has ordained them to be.

We are responsible for their safety and well being. Kids don't understand what is best for them. They are still growing mentally and physically.

Parents and adults should never bow down to the challenges of leading children down the right path. Teenagers may not appreciate or understand why parents and adults set boundaries. Years from now they will understand and appreciate boundaries kept them safe from harm. Parents and adults should never stop investigating who, what, when, where, why and how? before giving minors **Parental or Adult Consent!**

Your Legacy is a Gift to Earth with Everlasting Memories

Article VII:
Your Legacy is a Gift to Earth with Everlasting Memories

What do you want people to remember about you? What kind of impact do you want to have for years to come? When you use your gifts and talents to serve others you are building relationships. Relationships involve people caring about others. People will remember you for your gifts, talents, ideas, inventions, services or products you offered.

Legacy according to the Random House College Dictionary is anything handed down from the past, as from an ancestor or predecessor. Legacy could also be personal property, money, laws, customs and traditions. Many people feel it is an honor to continue the legacies passed down from their ancestors. It is important to leave something of value that will continue to benefit others after you expire from Earth. Your legacy will be the remnant that remains of you in the Earth.

When you leave a legacy, it shows your accomplishments during your lifetime. It gives a snap-shot of your goals, interests, talents and abilities. Your legacy shows what was dear to your heart while you lived on Earth. It shows what you were passionate about. Your legacy to Earth is usually a continuation of what people enjoyed while you lived. People continue to benefit from what you offered to Planet Earth.

Today we continue to benefit from the legacies of Dr. Martin Luther King, Jr. for his activism, ideas, speeches and marches to help in the Civil Rights Movement. Madame C. J. Walker left a legacy of the power of entrepreneurship. She is listed in the Guinness Book of Records as the first female of any race to become a self-made millionaire. Today we continue to enjoy the rags to riches story told about her life and the hair care products she manufactured.

According to Wikipedia.com, Karl Benz invented the first modern automobile in 1885. Henry Ford is remembered for maximizing on the assembly line technique in 1914. He manufactured the first affordable automobile called the Ford Model T in 1927. The invention of the modern automobile is still a major necessity in the United States and other countries around the world.

You can also leave a legacy of a good reputation that is associated with your name. According to the Bible in Proverbs 22:1, a good name is rather to be chosen than great riches, and loving favour rather than silver and gold. Martin Luther King Jr. is remembered also for his good name. He promoted and modeled peaceful demonstrations during the Civil Rights Movement. He also won the Nobel Peace Prize in 1964.

Planning, preparing and building your dreams goes hand in hand with your legacy. Whatever you build successfully remains in the Earth when you expire. The business and profits you leave can be passed down to your children, family members or friends.

Before you expire communicate to your family members how you want your legacy to continue. You can also re-communicate this in your Will. It is up to you to plan what you will leave and to whom. Your legacy will have everlasting memories from generation to generation. Your talents, gifts, ideas, inventions, services or products will continue to be used and appreciated by many.

About the Author

Brenda Diann Johnson was born in Dallas, Texas on September 14, 1970 to Robert Johnson and Thelma Byrd. She is the oldest of five children. She has a brother, sister, and two half brothers.

Brenda received her education from the Dallas and Wharton, Texas school systems. She graduated from Government, Law, and Law Enforcement Magnet High School in Dallas. She received her Bachelor of Arts degree in Communications (Broadcast News) from UTA in Arlington, Texas and her Masters of Education Degree from Strayer University. She has her Texas license in Life, Health, Accident & HMO insurance, her Texas Adjusters License in All Lines and she is a Texas Notary Public.

Today, Brenda is the CEO/Founder of The Young Scholar's Book Club and ASWIFTT ENTERPRISES, LLC. She is an experienced educator who has taught and tutored Pre-K through College. Brenda is the Dean of Education, Curriculum & Instruction for Best Practices Training Institute. (B.P.T.I.) She has also authored books and articles.

From 2001 to 2002, Brenda served as the chairperson for an entrepreneur group called STEP (Sowing Toward Everlasting Prosperity) and as the Potter's House Center Leader for the Plan Fund. Brenda also served as the Co-Founder of ASWIFTT Writer's Guild from 2010 to 2019.

In the community, Brenda has served as a volunteer to organizations that help AIDS, HIV, and Syphilis patients. Brenda currently lives in Texas with her family.

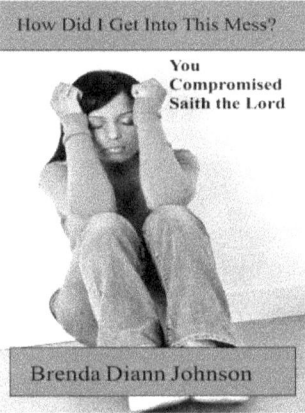

Services and Books

ASWIFTT ENTERPRISES, LLC

Business advertising for Print & Media
BOOK PUBLISHING
RADIO
T.V.
Newspaper
We have affordable advertising packages in our media categories. Some Ads are as low as $35.00. For information about our Business Ads and Commercials email us.

You can also visit us online or e-mail us:
www.aswifttbooks.com
aswifttbookpublishing@yahoo.com

ASWIFTT BOOKS

(Ambassadors Sent With Information For This Time)

ASWIFTT ENTERPRISES, LLC creates businesses that write and publish content in all three (3) media genres such as radio, t.v., and newspaper that focus on delivering timely, newsworthy and accurate news stories. The media genres also report on local, regional, national and international topics.

The Young Scholar's Workbook:
Book I Vol. I (www.tysbookclub.com)

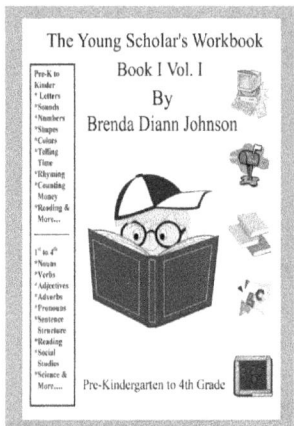

How Did I Get Into This Mess?
You Compromised, Saith the Lord
2nd Edition

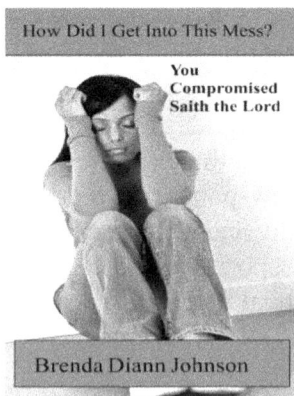

ASWIFTT ENTERPRISES, LLC ORDER FORM

Name_____

Address_____

City_____

State_____

Zip_____

Item _____**Amount**_____
Item _____**Amount**_____
Item _____**Amount**_____

Add $5.00 for Shipping and Handling on books
Total:_____

Make Checks, Money Orders, Cashier's Checks out to:

ASWIFTT ENTERPRISES, LLC

P.O. Box 380669

Duncanville, Texas 75138

Credit Card Orders:

Circle One: Master Card   Visa   American Express   Discover

Credit Card
Number_____

Exp. Date_____

61

Three Digit Security Number on back of
Card_____
Name & Address Associated with Credit Card:

_____

_____   _____

Authorization Signature   **Date**

Orders will be processed or shipped 2 to 4 weeks
from the date order is received. Direct concerns
on orders to: aswifttbookpublishing@yahoo.com

Thank you for your business! Make copies of this
form.

Bibliography

Bibliography

Books:

Authorized King James Version. Holy Bible. Grand
    Rapids: Zondervan Publishing House, 1994.

Random House, Inc. The Random House College
    Dictionary, Revised Edition. New York: Random
    House, Inc. 1988.

CD Sources:

Time: The Currency Of A Prosperous Life. CD.
    Common Sense Approach To Life With Randy
    Morrison, 3 CD Series.
www.commonsenseapproach.org

On-Line Sources:

Pavlina, Steve. "Overcoming Procrastination" Steve
Pavlina Articles. On-line. Internet. 19, Dec.
2011. Available:
http://www.stevepavlina.com/articles/overcoming-
procrastination.htm

Dictionary.com. On-line. "Works" Internet. 20, Dec.
2011. Available:
http://dictionary.reference.com/browse/works

Wikipedia.com. On-line. "Time Management" Internet. 20, Dec. 2011. Available: http://en.wikipedia.org/wiki/Time_management

Joshi, Kamla. "Success Formula! Avoid 10 Most Important Time Stealers" Bukisa June 2009. On-line. Internet. 10 Jan. 2012. Available: http://www.bukisa.com/articles/115044_success-formula-avoid-10-most-important-time-stealers

Garner, Eric. "Say No To Time Stealers" Articlesbase October 2007. On-line. Internet. 10 Jan. 2012. Available: http://www.articlesbase.com/self-improvement-articles/say-no-to-time-stealers-231138.html

Gallozzi, Chuck. "Personal Strengths and Weaknesses" Personal-Development.com November 2009. On-line. Internet. 10 Jan. 2012. Available: http://www.personal-development.com/chuck/strengths-weaknesses.htm

Cole, William. "Is Selfishness Healthy?" Articlesbase August 2008. On-line. Internet. 10 Feb. 2012. Available: http://www.articlesbase.com/self-help-articles/is-selfishness-healthy-505748.html

Davis, Jeanie. "10 Parenting Tips for Raising Teenagers" WebMD.com August 2003. On-line. Internet. 10 Feb. 2012. Available: http://www.webmd.com/parenting/features/10-parenting-tips-for-raising-teenagers?page=2